Yajuj and Majuj

Muhyi'd-din 'Abd al-Hamid

Dar al-Taqwa

ISBN 1 870582 60 8

Translation: Aisha Bewley

Editors: Abdalhaqq Bewley and Muhammad Isa Waley

Production: Bookwork

Published by:
    Dar Al Taqwa Ltd.
    7A Melcombe Street
    Baker Street
    London NW1 6AE

Printed and bound in Great Britain by
DELUXE PRINTERS
London NW10 7NR.

Table of Contents

In the name of God, most Gracious, most Merciful

Preface

Praise belongs to Allah. We praise Him and seek His help and ask His forgiveness and turn to Him. We seek refuge with Allah from the evils of our selves and our bad deeds. *"Anyone Allah guides, he is truly guided. But as for anyone He misguides, you will find no protector to give them right guidance."* (18:17)

Praise and blessings be upon him who was sent as a mercy to all beings, our master Muhammad, and on his family and Companions, and may Allah grant them peace. Amen.

Belief in the Unseen is one of the fundamentals and pillars of faith and no one's faith complete until he believes in this dimension of existence which is hidden from us. The Resurrection of the Dead with its attendant terrors is an integral part of the Islamic creed, as is belief in the Last Day with all its signs, terrors and portents. Some of the signs of the Last Hour and its greatest terrors were made clear to us by the Messenger of Allah, may Allah bless him and grant him peace, in a *hadith* related by Hudhayfa ibn Usayd, may Allah be pleased with him. He said, "The Last Hour will not arrive before you have seen ten signs announcing it." He then mentioned the Smoke, the Dajjal, the Beast, the rising of the sun from its place of setting, the descent of 'Isa son of Maryam, Yajuj and Majuj (Gog and Magog), three subsidences of the earth - one in the east, one in the west and one in the Arabian Peninsula - and that after that a fire would spread from Yemen and drive people to their place of gathering. (Related by Muslim and Abu Dawud)

This book will deal mainly with Yajuj and Majuj and examine what can be said about this category of Allah's creatures. We will

1

clarify their number, their location, the story of their connection with Dhu'l-Qarnayn and the fact that they will emerge before the Beast arrives. We will describe their clothing, food and drink and then those signs which occur after Yajuj and Majuj appear, turning our attention in all of this to what the people of knowledge and Qur'anic commentators have said.

I ask Allah, the High and Powerful, that this work may be sincerely for the sake of His Noble Face and I ask Him to reward all who participated and helped in publishing this book and in spreading good among the Muslims; and I also ask Him to seal our lives with the seal of the righteous. Allah has the power to do whatever He wills and is able to answer our prayers.

O Allah, bless our master Muhammad and his family and Companions. Amen.

Praise belongs to Allah, the Lord of all the worlds.

Muhyi'd-din 'Abd al-Hamid

Chapter One

Yajuj and Majuj according to the Qur'an and *Sunna*

Yajuj and Majuj in the Qur'an:

The Almighty says:

"When Yajuj and Majuj are let loose and swarm down from every slope, and the True Promise is very close, the eyes of those who rejected will be transfixed: 'Alas for us! We were heedless of this! No, truly we were wrong-doers.'" (21:96-97)

"Then he followed a path until he arrived between the two mountains where he found a people scarcely able to understand speech. They said, 'O Dhu'l-Qarnayn! Yajuj and Majuj are causing corruption in the land. Can we, therefore, pay tribute to you in return for your constructing a barrier between us and them?' He said, 'The power my Lord has granted me is better than that. Just give me a robust helping hand and I will build a solid wall between you and them. Bring me ingots of iron!' Then, when he had made it level between the two high mountain-sides, he said, 'Blow!' and when he had made it all a red-hot fire, he said, 'Bring me molten brass to pour on it.' Thereafter they were unable to climb over it nor could they make a breach in it." (18:92-97)

Yajuj and Majuj in the *Sunna*

Sayyidatuna Zaynab bint Jahsh, may Allah be pleased with her, said that the Messenger of Allah, may Allah bless him and grant him peace, said, "There is no god but Allah. Woe to the Arabs from an evil which is drawing near! Today a breach has been made in the wall of Yajuj and Majuj this big," and he made a circle with his thumb and forefinger. (Another variant says that he indicated seventy or ninety). She asked, "O Messenger of Allah, will we be destroyed if there are righteous people among us?" He said, "Yes, if there is abundant wickedness." (al-Bukhari)

An-Nawwas ibn Sam'an, may Allah be pleased with him, narrated that the Prophet, may Allah bless him and grant him peace, said: "Allah will reveal to 'Isa, 'I have brought forth some slaves of Mine whom no one will able to fight, so take My slaves to the Mountain for protection.' Allah will send forth Yajuj and Majuj and *'they will swarm down from every slope'*." (Muslim)

According to Hudhayfa ibn Usayd, may Allah be pleased with him, the Prophet, may Allah bless him and grant him peace, said, "The Last Hour will not arrive before you have seen ten signs announcing it," and he mentioned Yajuj and Majuj among them. (Muslim)

'Abdullah ibn Mas'ud, may Allah be pleased with him, stated: "When the Messenger of Allah, may Allah bless him and grant him peace, went on his Night Journey, he met Ibrahim, Musa, and 'Isa, peace be upon them, and they discussed the Last Hour," and the narrative continues until he said, "They let 'Isa speak, peace be upon him, and he mentioned the slaying of the Dajjal. Then he said, 'After that the people will return to their lands and will be met by Yajuj and Majuj *"swarm down from every slope."*'" (Ahmad ibn Hanbal and al-Hakim)

Abu Hurayra, may Allah be pleased with him, narrated that the Prophet, may Allah bless him and grant him peace, said, "They will come out against people and drink all the water, and people will flee from them. They will shoot their arrows into the sky and

4

they will come back blood-stained. They will say, 'We have defeated the people of the earth and we are superior to those in heaven in strength and might." (at-Tirmidhi, al-Hakim and Ibn Maja)

Abu Hurayra, may Allah be pleased with him, narrated that the Messenger of Allah, may Allah bless him and grant him peace, said, "Yajuj and Majuj will pour down the slopes every day until they seem like the rays of the sun." (Ahmad ibn Hanbal)

Abu Sa'id al-Khudri, may Allah be pleased with him, narrated: "I heard the Messenger of Allah, Messenger of Allah, say, 'Yajuj and Majuj will be let loose and they will emerge as Allah Almighty has declared: *they swarm down from every slope.*'" (Muslim)

Harmala, may Allah be pleased with him, narrated that his aunt narrated, "The Messenger of Allah, may Allah bless him and grant him peace, once made a speech when he had his finger bandaged because of a scorpion sting and said, 'You say that you have no enemy. But you will continue to have enemies to fight until Yajuj and Majuj emerge with broad faces, small eyes, and reddish brown skins, *swarming down from every slope*'." (Ahmad ibn Hanbal)

The prayer of 'Isa ibn Maryam against Yajuj and Majuj

It is established in numerous *hadiths* that the Dajjal will wreak havoc in the earth and will tempt people and call people to worship him instead of Allah. These trials and afflictions will continue until the Messiah, son of Maryam, peace be upon him, descends at the White Minbar east of Damascus, wearing two dyed garments, with his arms supported on the wings of two angels. He will pursue the Dajjal and catch him and kill him at the eastern gate of Ludd[1].

---

1. Meaning somewhere in Syria or Palestine.

5

The Prophet, may Allah bless him and grant him peace, said: "Allah Almighty will reveal to 'Isa, 'I have brought forth some slaves of Mine whom no one will be able to fight, so take My slaves to the Mountain for protection.' Then Allah Almighty will send Yajuj and Majuj as He says, '*When Yajuj and Majuj are let loose and swarm down from every slope.*' (21:96) Then 'Isa, peace be upon him, and his Companions will pray to Allah, who will send them worms in their necks and they will die as in a single breath..." (Muslim)

According to the *hadith* related from Ibn Mas'ud about the Night journey 'Isa said, "Allah will destroy the Dajjal when he sees me and then people will return to their lands and homelands." He continued, "Then Yajuj and Majuj will emerge, swarming down from every slope, trampling on their lands and destroying everything they come across. Whenever they come to any water, they will drink it up. Then people will return to their homelands complaining about them. I will pray to Allah against them and He will destroy them and cause them to die." (Ahmad ibn Hanbal and Ibn Maja)

Chapter Two

Dhu'l-Qarnayn and Yajuj and Majuj

The story of Dhu'l-Qarnayn is mentioned in the Noble Qur'an, which tells us extraordinary things about him and how Allah opened the way for him and established him on the earth and gave him the means, method and knowledge to do everything. But in particular there is the remarkable way he dealt with the people who were being persecuted by Yajuj and Majuj and whose lives were being made intolerable by them. Those weak people had no one to turn to but this righteous man and they begged his assistance in keeping Yajuj and Majuj at bay. So he came to their aid and responded to their pleas by building an immense defensive wall with strong foundations which Yajuj and Majuj could not climb because of its great height and the slipperiness of its surface; nor could they could not breach it, because of the strength of its construction and the firmness of its foundations. Through him, then, Allah removed the evil of Yajuj and Majuj and prevented them from tyrannising that persecuted people.

The Story of Dhu'l-Qarnayn in the Noble Qur'an

Allah Almighty says:

> *"They will ask you about Dhu'l-Qarnayn. Say: 'I will relate an account of him to you.' We gave him power and authority on the earth and granted him a way to everything. So he followed a way until he reached the setting of*

7

*the sun and found it setting in a muddy spring, and found
a people beside it. We said, 'Dhu'l-Qarnayn! You may
either punish them or treat them with gentleness.' He said,
'As for anyone who does wrong, we shall punish him and
then he will be returned to his Lord and He will punish
him with a dreadful penalty. But as for anyone who
believes and acts rightly, he shall receive the best of
rewards and we shall issue a command, making things
easy for him.'*

*"Then he followed a way until he reached the rising of
the sun and found it rising on a people to whom We had
not given any shelter from it. Thus Our knowledge encom-
passes all that happened to him.*

*"Then he followed a path until he arrived between the
two mountains where he found a people scarcely able to
understand speech. They said, 'O Dhu'l-Qarnayn! Yajuj
and Majuj are causing corruption in the land. Can we,
therefore, pay tribute to you in return for your constructing a barrier between us and them?' He said, 'The power
my Lord has granted me is better than that. Just give me a
robust helping hand and I will build a solid wall between
you and them. Bring me ingots of iron!' Then, when he
had made it level between the two high mountainsides, he
said, 'Blow!' and when he had made it all a red hot fire,
he said, 'Bring me molten brass to pour on it.' Thereafter
they were unable to climb over it nor could they make a
breach in it. He said, 'This is a mercy from my Lord. But
when my Lord's promise comes about, He will crush it flat.
The promise of my Lord is surely true.'*

*"We will abandon them, that Day, to pound against
each other in surging waves and the Trumpet will be
blown and We will gather them all together."* (18:83-99)

We can see from these *ayats* of the Noble Qur'an that Allah
Almighty has praised Dhu'l-Qarnayn for his great journeys to the
east and west and for his conquest and just rulership of vast
regions of the earth.

The identity of Dhu'l-Qarnayn

Different things are said as to who Dhu'l-Qarnayn was. Some people say that he was simply a just king, others that he was a Prophet, and others that he was a Messenger.

The opinion of the Caliph 'Umar ibn al-Khattab

One man was heard to say to another, "Dhu'l-Qarnayn!" 'Umar said, "What! Are you not content to give yourselves the names of Prophets so that you must give yourselves the angels' names!" (Al-Ghazzali, *Ihya' 'ulum ad-din*)

The opinion of Ibn 'Abbas

Ibn 'Abbas says that Dhu'l-Qarnayn was a righteous king with whose deeds Allah was pleased and whom He praised in His Book. He was victorious and al-Khidr was his minister. Ibn 'Abbas mentioned that al-Khidr, peace be upon him, was at the head of Dhu'l-Qarnayn's army and that he held the position of adviser to him.

The opinion of al-Azraqi

According to al-Azraqi, Dhu'l-Qarnayn became Muslim through Ibrahim the Friend, peace be upon him, and performed *tawaf* of the Noble Ka'ba with him and with Isma'il.

'Ubayd ibn 'Umayr and his son

They said that Dhu'l-Qarnayn went on *hajj* on foot and Ibrahim met him and prayed for him and liked him; and that Allah subjected the clouds to him to carry him wherever he wished.

'Ali ibn Abi Talib

'Ali said, "He was neither a Prophet nor a Messenger nor an angel, but a righteous servant of Allah."

The reason why he was called Dhu'l-Qarnayn

In Arabic the name Dhu'l-Qarnayn means "the Possessor of Two Horns" and it is said that he was given it because he had something resembling two horns on his head. It is the opinion of some writers that it was a metaphorical title because he was the king of both Persia and Greece. Other people say that it he was called that because he reached the horns of the sun in the west and east and ruled the land between them. Al-Hasan al-Basri said that he had two locks of hair on his head and was called Dhu'l-Qarnayn for that reason. 'Ali ibn Abi Talib was asked about Dhu'l-Qarnayn and said, "He was a servant who was faithful to Allah and so He was faithful to him. He called his people, but they struck him on his horn and he died. Then Allah brought him to life and he called his people to Allah, but they struck him on his other horn and he died and so he is called Dhu'l-Qarnayn."

His lineage

He was from the Yemeni tribe of Himyar and his mother was Greek. He was called the 'son of the philosopher' because of his great intelligence. The Himyarites boast of that and say about their ancestor:

Dhu'l-Qarnayn was our Muslim ancestor,
a king whom other kings obeyed and to whom they rallied.
He travelled to the furthest east and the furthest west
seeking the means of command from a guided sage.

He saw the place where the setting sun descends
in the spring of Dhi Kalb and Tha'ti Harq.
After him came Bilqis who was his aunt.
She ruled over them until the hoopoe came.

Dhu'l-Qarnayn and the construction of the wall

Most of the opinions of the commentators regarding Dhu'l-Qarnayn are similar. They state that he was a righteous man but not a Prophet. He was faithful to Allah and Allah was well-disposed towards him. Allah gave him the means, power, ability and resources to enable him to rule the east and the west. He reached the place where the sun sets, meaning the west, and its people obeyed him and he reached the place where the sun rises, meaning the east, and its people obeyed him, and he also reached the place between the two mountains. This is said to be located between Armenia and Azerbaijan according to one opinion. It is also said to be between Samarqand and India. Allah knows best where it was actually located. There were some weak downtrodden people there who could not speak properly and had no means of livelihood or self-defence. Yajuj and Majuj had abased them by their strength and might and consumed their food, both fresh and dried, drank all their water, and imposed an evil punishment on them.

They asked the help of Dhu'l Qarnayn who clearly possessed strength and power and the means to save them from the devastating evil and dreadful affliction under which they toiled. With courtesy and modesty they requested him to construct a barrier between them and Yajuj and Majuj to protect them and defend them against this affliction. In return for that, they would collect a large amount of wealth for him, or, according to one statement, a share of the produce of their land. But because Dhu'l Qarnayn was an abstinent and righteous man, he told them that the blessing, wealth, resources and victories Allah had given him were better than what they offered him.

Nonetheless he agreed to their request to save them provided that they helped him by providing him with strong men as workers and skilful artisans. They went swiftly to work, bringing wood, coal, and pieces of iron. Allah guided him to place coal and wood between each two layers of iron. Then when the structure had been built up level with the peaks of the two mountains, he asked them to kindle fire and the wood and coal were lit so that the space between the layers of iron became empty. Then he brought molten brass and poured it over the iron and it filled the gaps between the iron layers and the iron became one smooth mass.

When Yajuj and Majuj tried to climb the wall they could not do so because of its smoothness and great height. They tried to pierce it from underneath but were unable to do so because of its hardness and the firmness of its foundations.

After Allah had accomplished this blessed deed and fulfilled His blessing upon those persecuted people by protecting them from the tyranny of Yajuj and Majuj, we find that Dhu'l-Qarnayn thanked his Lord and Master and acknowledged His bounty and praise and mercy and guidance. He said, *"This is a mercy from my Lord."* (18:98) He did not forget the Next World or the encounter with Allah or His promise. He said, *"But when my Lord's promise comes about, He will crush it flat. The promise of my Lord is surely true."* (18:98) In other words, in comparison with the strength, power and might of Allah, this immense unassailable wall was worthless and would be reduced to dust, level with the earth.

Allah showed mercy to Dhu'l-Qarnayn and he was a model of righteousness for people in respect of his humility, mercy and obedience to the commands of Allah Almighty, punishing evildoers for their evil and rewarding the good doers for their good. He filled the earth with justice after it had been full of injustice and he defended the weak and poor and stopped them being harmed. He stood firm against the people of corruption and misguidance and built a great barrier to keep them back and avert the harm they cause.

Chapter Three

Yajuj and Majuj are human beings

Abu Sa'id said that the Messenger of Allah, may Allah bless him and grant him peace, said, "Allah Almighty will say on the Day of Rising, 'Arise, Adam, and bring forth those among your offspring who are for the Fire.' He will ask, 'O Lord. who are those who are for the Fire?' Allah will reply, 'Nine hundred and ninety-nine of every thousand are for the Fire and one is for the Garden.' Then children will become white-haired and *every pregnant woman will abort the contents of her womb. You will see people drunk, yet they are not drunk, but the punishment of Allah is severe.*' (22:2)" They said, "Messenger of Allah, is that 'one' from among us?" The Messenger of Allah, may Allah bless him and grant him peace, said. "Rejoice in the good news that there is one of you for every thousand of Yajuj and Majuj."

Statements of scholars and commentators about Yajuj and Majuj

Most scholars and commentators agree that Yajuj and Majuj are descended from Adam and Hawwa but state that their form and character differ to a certain extent from the rest of mankind. It is in their nature to wreak havoc in the earth and destroy crops and herds and to be jealous of their neighbours, and it is in their blood to inflict harm on all creatures in the earth and in heaven.

13

Allah used His righteous servant Dhu'l-Qarnayn to prevent and repel their harm from people by building a barrier to hold them back. They will not overcome it until the promise of Allah Almighty comes about before the Last Hour – at which time they will emerge, ruining all the land, fertile and arid, and drinking dry the waters of all the seas and rivers they encounter.

Allah will use His righteous servant and Prophet, 'Isa ibn Maryam, peace be upon him and his mother, to lead the group of believers who have survived the trial of the Dajjal to safety. He will lead them to Mount Tur, where people will implore him to pray and intercede with Allah on their behalf to save them from Yajuj and Majuj. 'Isa will pray to his Lord and Allah will answer him and send against Yajuj and Majuj worms which will kill them. Their carcasses will fill the earth and the stench from them will fill every house. Then the people will go to 'Isa ibn Maryam and ask him to pray and intercede with Allah to save them from that new affliction.

'Isa will pray to his Lord and Allah Almighty will send birds with necks like camels who will pick up the corpses and carry them to the sea. Then Allah will send down rain from heaven and the earth will be cleansed of their stench. Allah will relieve the lands and people of the world of the harm of Yajuj and Majuj by the hand of 'Isa son of Maryam, peace be upon him. People will return to their houses and bring out their cattle thanking Allah Almighty for saving them from that affliction which had consumed everything fresh and dry and had destroyed crops and flocks. In this way the believers will be saved.

Chapter Four

Signs and Portents before the Appearance of Yajuj and Majuj

The *hadiths* of the Prophet, may Allah bless him and grant him peace, quoted previously, mention the appearance of certain signs and portents before the appearance of Yajuj and Majuj, although it is clear that there is no sequential order in their appearance because of the difference between the many transmissions as to which signs appear first and which follow.

The main signs presaging the appearance of Yajuj and Majuj are:

- The rising of the sun from the west.
- The Smoke.
- The Beast.
- The Dajjal.
- The descent of 'Isa ibn Maryam.
- 'Isa ibn Maryam killing the Dajjal.

Other subsidiary signs are:

- Fighting the Turks.
- Fighting the people of Ghur and Kirman,
- A group of the community of the Prophet Muhammad, may Allah bless him and grant him peace, remaining firm in the truth so that they fight the Jews and unbelievers and are helped in that by the stones and trees.

- The appearance of about thirty false messiahs claiming prophethood.

The *hadiths* also mention the following signs:

- The disappearance of knowledge and the spread of ignorance.
- The spread of fornication and wine drinking.
- Many women and few men.
- Time passing rapidly.
- Good actions decreasing.
- Widespread avarice.
- The appearance of civil strife.
- Bloodshed becoming rife.

There are many *hadiths* of the Prophet, may Allah bless him and grant him peace, which speak about these signs. A selection of them are presented here:

Muslim related from Hudhayfa, may Allah be pleased with him, that the Messenger of Allah, may Allah bless him and grant him peace, said: "The Last Hour will not arrive before you have seen ten signs announcing it." He then mentioned the Smoke, the Dajjal, the Beast, the rising of the sun from its place of setting, the descent of 'Isa son of Maryam, Yajuj and Majuj, three subsidences - one in the east, one in the west and one in the Arabian Peninsula - and that after that a fire would spread from Yemen and drive people to their place of gathering.

Abu Hurayra, may Allah be pleased with him, narrated that the Messenger of Allah, may Allah bless him and grant him peace, said: "Time will pass rapidly and good deeds will decrease. Avarice will be cast into the hearts and trials will appear and there will be much *harj*." They asked, "O Messenger of Allah, what is that?" He replied, "Killing. Killing." (al-Bukhari)

Abu Hurayra, may Allah be pleased with him, narrated that the Messenger of Allah, may Allah bless him and grant him peace, said: "The Last Hour will not come until my community goes the way of the generations before them." (al-Bukhari)

Abu'l-Yaman related from Shu'ayb from Abu'z-Zinad from 'Abdu'r-Rahman from Abu Hurayra, may Allah be pleased with him, that the Messenger of Allah, may Allah bless him and grant him peace, said, "The Last Hour will not come until two large parties who follow the same call fight a large battle; until about thirty false messiahs appear, each claiming to be the Messenger of Allah; until knowledge is taken away; there will be many earthquakes; time will pass quickly; seditions will appear; there will be much *harj*, which means killing; there will be much wealth among you and it will be so excessive that a man with wealth will worry about finding someone to take his *sadaqa*, so that he offers it and the person to whom he offers it says, 'I have no need of it'; men will compete with one another in constructing tall buildings; a man will pass by a man's grave and say, 'Would that I were in his place!'; and the sun will rise from the West. When it rises and people see it, they will all believe, but - *'Then any belief a self has will bring it no benefit if it did not believe before or earn good in its belief.'* (6;158) The Last Hour will come while two men are spreading out their garment but before they can sell it or fold it up. The Last Hour will come when a man has milked his she-camel and has taken the milk but before he is able to taste it. The Last Hour will come while a man is repairing a water-basin but before he can put water into it. The Last Hour will come when a person has lifted a morsel of food to his mouth but before he can eat it." (al-Bukhari)

Ibn Mas'ud, may Allah be pleased with him, narrated that the Messenger of Allah, may Allah bless him and grant him peace, observed, "The Last Hour will not come until every tribe is led by its hypocrites." (at-Tabarani)

Abu Hurayra, may Allah be pleased with him, narrated that the Messenger of Allah, may Allah bless him and grant him peace, said, "The Last Hour will not come until the leader of a people is the worst of them and their deviants lead their clans." (at-Tirmidhi)

Abu Hurayra, may Allah be pleased with him, narrated that the Messenger of Allah, may Allah bless him and grant him peace, said, "When authority lies with others than those who should rightfully have it, then expect the Last Hour." (al-Bukhari)

Ibn Mas'ud, may Allah be pleased with him, reported that the Messenger of Allah, may Allah bless him and grant him peace, said, "The Last Hour will not come until children are an annoyance and the rain fails and the days rush past." (at-Tabarani)

Abu Dharr, may Allah be pleased with him, narrated that the Messenger of Allah, may Allah bless him and grant him peace, said, "The Last Hour will not come until the Muslims fight the Jews and the Muslims will kill them until every Jew tries to hide behind a rock." (Muslim)

Anas, may Allah be pleased with him, narrated that the Messenger of Allah, may Allah bless him and grant him peace, said: "There will be deceitful years before the Dajjal in which the truthful will lie and the liar will be truthful, and in which the trustworthy will be treacherous and the treacherous trustworthy, and in which the contemptible will speak out." (Ahmad ibn Hanbal and Abu Ya'la)

Abu Hurayra, may Allah be pleased with him, reported that the Messenger of Allah, may Allah bless him and grant him peace, declared, "This community will not vanish before a man goes to a woman and has intercourse with her in the road and the best of them on that day will say, 'If only he had concealed it from us behind the wall." (Abu Ya'la)

According to Thawban, may Allah be pleased with him, the Messenger of Allah, may Allah bless him and grant him peace, said, "The Last Hour will not come until some of the tribes of my community join the idolaters and some tribes of my community worship idols." (Muslim and Ahmad ibn Hanbal)

Jabir ibn 'Abdullah, may Allah be pleased with him, stated that he heard the Messenger of Allah, may Allah bless him and grant him peace, say, "There will be liars before the Last Hour, one of whom will be the master of Yamama, and the master of San'at al-'Abasi. One of them will be the master of Himyar, and another will be the Dajjal, who is the greatest trial." (Ahmad ibn Hanbal)

The Prophet, peace and blessings be upon him, said, "The Last Hour will not come until 'Isa son of Maryam descends as a fair ruler and just Imam, breaks the crosses, kills the pigs, abolishes the *jizya,* and is so lavish in distributing wealth that there is no one to accept it." (Ahmad ibn Hanbal and Ibn Maja)

Chapter Five

Signs and Portents after the destruction of Yajuj and Majuj

There are also many *hadiths* relating the signs and portents after the appearance of Yajuj and Majuj:

According to the *hadith* narrated from Hudhayfa ibn Usayd, may Allah be pleased with him, the Messenger of Allah, may Allah bless him and grant him peace, said, "The Hour will not arrive before you have seen ten signs announcing it." He then mentioned the Smoke, the Dajjal, the Beast, the rising of the sun from its place of setting, the descent of 'Isa son of Maryam, Yajuj and Majuj, three subsidences - one in the east, one in the west and one in the Arabian peninsula - and that after that a fire would spread from Yemen and drive people to their place of gathering. (Muslim)

This would seem to indicate that the subsidences and fire are signs that will occur after Yajuj and Majuj.

Ibn 'Amr, may Allah be pleased with him, said that the Messenger of Allah, may Allah bless him and grant him peace, said, "There will be much emigration and the best land for the best people of the earth will be that to which Ibrahim, peace be upon him, emigrated. The world's evil people, whose words please them but are ugly in the sight of Allah, will remain where they were. The fire will force them together with the apes and pigs. It will spend the night with them wherever they spend the night and midday with them wherever they pass midday and it will consume those who fall behind." (Ahmad ibn Hanbal)

21

Emigration to the land of the gathering and the emergence of the fire and its assembling people and driving them are among the signs which will appear after the emergence of Yajuj and Majuj.

Ibn 'Umar, may Allah be pleased with him, said that the Messenger of Allah, may Allah bless him and grant him peace, said, "Fire will emerge from Hadramawt, or in Hadramawt, before the Day of Rising and force people together." They asked, "Messenger of Allah, what do you command us to do?" He said, "You should go to Syria." (Ahmad ibn Hanbal)

Hudhayfa ibn al-Yaman, may Allah be pleased with him, narrated that the Messenger of Allah, may Allah bless him and grant him peace, said, "The fire which is now dormant will head for you in a valley called Barhut. People will be encompassed by its punishment, which will consume people and property and go right round the world in eight days. Wind and clouds will disappear. Its heat during the night will be greater than the heat you experience during the day. It will make a noise between heaven and earth like crashing thunder." He was asked, "Messenger of Allah, will believing men and women be safe on that day?" He replied, "Where will the believing men and women be on that day? Worse than donkeys, copulating as animals copulate – and there will not be one man among them who says, 'Stop! Stop!'" (at-Tabarani)

Abu Hurayra, may Allah be pleased with him, said that the Messenger of Allah, may Allah bless him and grant him peace, said, "People will be gathered in three groups: those who hope for the Garden and fear the Fire; those who come with two on a camel up to ten on a camel; and the fire will drive the rest of them together. It will spend midday with them wherever they spend midday and spend the night with them wherever they spend the night. It will stay with them morning and evening." (al-Bukhari and Muslim)

Sulayman ibn Dawud related from 'Imran from Qatada from 'Abdullah ibn Abi 'Uqba that Sa'd reported that the Messenger of Allah, may Allah bless him and grant him peace, said. "*Hajj* and *'Umra* will be made to this House after the emergence of Yajuj and Majuj." (Ahmad ibn Hanbal)

The summary of these signs and portents which will take place after the appearance of Yajuj and Majuj according to most statements is that there will be a subsidence of the earth in the east and one in the west and one in the Arabian Peninsula, and a fire issuing from Yemen or Hadramawt which will drive people to the place of gathering in Syria.

We ask Allah to protect us from all trials, both manifest and hidden, and to make us believers declaring His Unity before the coming of the Final Hour. Amen. Amen.

Chapter Six

Yajuj and Majuj

The origin of their name

It is said that "Ya'juj and Ma'juj" are non-Arab names, like Harut and Marut. According to another opinion, however, they are Arab names in which case they must be based on Arabic roots. Following this opinion it is said that Ya'juj is derived from the verb *ajja*, which means to burn fiercely, or that it comes from the noun *ujaj* which means to be very salty and to burn because of it. It is also said that it comes from the noun *ajj* which means a swift enemy. Ma'juj is said to derive from the verb *maja* which means to be in tumult. The names are also sometimes read as Yajuj and Majuj without a *hamza*, in which case their two roots are thought to be *yajja*, of unknown meaning, and *majja* which means to spit out.

Their identity and description

Most scholars say that Yajuj and Majuj are human beings descended fromAdam and Hawwa; but a few say that they are descendants of Adam but not of Hawwa. There is no evidence for this position and it is not acceptable. Ibn Hajar replies to them by saying, "None of the early Muslims held this opinion except Ka'b al-Ahbar, and he is refuted by the *hadith*, 'They are from among the descendants of Nuh,' because Nuh was one of the descendants of Adam and Hawwa'."

Ibn Kathir states in *al-Bidaya wa an-Nihaya* that they are the descendants of Yafith (Japeth), the father of the Turks. Yafith was a son of Nuh, peace be upon him. Ibn Kathir said in the same book that they are people who have the racial characteristics of the Turks, with small eyes, flat noses, and reddish hair and the same stature and colour. Anyone who claims that some of them are as tall as palm-trees and that others are square and that still others have huge ears has delved into something about which he has no knowledge, and Allah knows best.

Al-Qurtubi mentioned in the *Kitab at-Tadhkira* that 'Abdu'l-Malik said that they are two nations descended from Yafith, son of Nuh. Allah has given them such long life and abundant offspring that a man of Yajuj and Majuj does not die until he has sired a thousand children. If all the sons of Adam were to be divided into ten parts, Yajuj and Majuj would comprise nine-tenths of them and the rest of the children of Adam one tenth. Al-Qurtubi also mentioned that 'Ali said, "Some of them are a span tall and they have claws and fangs like wild beasts. They call one another, cooing like doves, and sleep with animals and bay like wolves. They have a lot of hair which protects them from heat and cold." He also said that ad-Dahhak said, "They are a people of the Turks."

Ibn 'Abbas, may Allah be pleased with him and his father, said that the earth was divided into six parts: five parts for Yajuj and Majuj and one part for everyone else. Muqatal said, "They are the descendants of Yafith, son of Nuh, peace be upon him."

'Abdu'r-Razzaq transmits from Qatada that Yajuj and Majuj consist of twenty-two tribes. Dhu'l-Qarnayn built a wall, holding back twenty-one of them. One tribe had gone out on a raid and remained outside the wall. They are called Turks because they were left (*turikat*) outside the wall.

To sum up the various opinions, they are normal people and their physique, height, and shape varies. They were created from Adam and Hawwa' from the descendants of Yafith, son of Nuh. They have long nails and teeth and thick hair. They call each other,

26

cooing like doves, and they sleep together like beasts. They comprise nine-tenths of the earth's population and take up five-sixths of its surface area. And Allah knows best.

Their location

Most of the *tafsirs* have related that they live between Armenia and Azerbaijan but it is also said that they live between India and Samarqand. And Allah knows best.

Their ruining the earth

Allah Almighty says:

"Then he followed a path until he arrived between the two mountains where he found a people scarcely able to understand speech. They said, 'O Dhu'l-Qarnayn! Yajuj and Majuj are causing corruption in the land. Can we, therefore, pay tribute to you in return for your making a barrier between us and them?' " (18:92-94)

Scholars disagree about what "causing corruption" means. Some of them say that they used to kill people. Others say that they used to eat human flesh. It is said that if they came out in the springtime and found crops growing, they would eat them, and if they found any dry food, they would carry it off. They had no qualms about stealing, looting and raping and inflicting every sort of harm and injury to those in their way.

When they come out at the end of time, they will not pass any building without destroying it or any food without eating it or any water without drinking it dry. Then they will say, "We have slaughtered the people of the earth. Let us now slaughter those in heaven!" They will shoot their arrows towards the sky and Allah will return their arrows to them stained with blood.

The significance of their appearance

Yajuj and Majuj will emerge at the end of time and their emergence will be one of the chief signs of the Last Hour. Allah Almighty says:

"When Yajuj and Majuj are let loose and swarm down from every slope; and the True Promise is very close, the eyes of those who rejected will be transfixed: 'Alas for us! We were heedless of this! No, truly we were wrongdoers.'" (21:96-97)

The Almighty also says:

"Then he followed a path until he arrived between the two mountains where he found a people scarcely able to understand speech. They said, 'O Dhu'l-Qarnayn! Yajuj and Majuj are causing corruption in the land. Can we, therefore, pay tribute to you in return for your making a barrier between us and them?'" (18:92-94)

These *ayats* indicate the existence of Yajuj and Majuj and their emergence at the end of time. Then Allah will give them permission to breach the wall constructed by Dhu'l-Qarnayn and to emerge from behind it to destroy people and ruin their lives – but they will not be able to complete their task because Allah will ensure that 'Isa, peace be upon him, takes the remaining believers to Mount Sinai. Then Allah will send worms against the hordes of Yajuj and Majuj and destroy them. The earth will reek of their stench, and then Allah will send rains to sweep them and cleanse the earth of them.

Their connection with Dhu'l-Qarnayn

Allah Almighty says:

"Then he followed a path until he arrived between the two mountains where he found a people scarcely able to understand speech. They said, 'O Dhu'l-Qarnayn! Yajuj and Majuj are causing corruption in the land. Can we, therefore, pay tribute to you in return for your making a barrier between us and them?' He said, 'The power my Lord has granted me is better than that. Just give me a robust helping hand and I will build a solid wall between you and them.'" (18:92-95)

This has already been gone over in some detail earlier in the book but it is important to remember that this incident provides us with a significant amount of what we know about Yajuj and Majuj.

Their breaching the wall and coming forth

Abu Hurayra, may Allah be pleased with him, said that the Messenger of Allah, may Allah bless him and grant him peace, said, "Every day Yajuj and Majuj are digging and when they can almost see daylight on the other side, the one in charge of them says, 'Return and finish it tomorrow.' Then Allah makes the wall as strong as it was before. This will continue until the time comes for them to emerge and Allah desires to let them loose against mankind. They will dig and when they can almost see daylight on the other side, the one in charge will say, 'Return and finish it tomorrow if Allah wills.' But when they return the wall will be as they left it. So they will dig it and emerge against mankind. They will drink up all the water and people will barricade themselves against them in fortresses. They will shoot their arrows towards heaven and they will return blood-stained to them. They will say,

'We have conquered the people of the earth and overcome the people of heaven.' Then Allah will send worms in their necks which will kill them."

The Messenger of Allah, may Allah bless him and grant him peace, said: "By the One Who has my soul in His hand, the beasts of the earth will become fat and thankful for the great amount of their flesh that is eaten." (Ibn Maja)

Ka'b al-Ahbar said, "Yajuj and Majuj are attacking the wall with their axes until they are almost through. Then they will say, 'We shall resume tomorrow,' and the wall will return to its former state. However, when the command comes, they will add 'and finish the job, Allah willing' to their words, 'We will resume tomorrow,' and when they return to it, it will be as they left it. They will breach it and emerge. The first of them will come to a lake and drink up all the water in it. Then the middle group of them will come to it and will lick up the mud in it. The last of them will come and say, 'There used to be water here.' Then they will shoot their arrows towards heaven and say, 'We have conquered those in the earth and we have overcome those in heaven.' Allah will afflict them with worm-like creatures which will attack their necks and kill them so that the earth reeks with the stench of their bodies. Then Allah will send birds who will carry their bodies to the sea. Allah will release rain from heaven for forty days and the earth will produce its blessings and good things to such an extent that a single pomegranate is sufficient to feed a whole household."

Abu Sa'id al-Khudri, may Allah be pleased with him, narrated that the Messenger of Allah, may Allah bless him and grant him peace, said, "Yajuj and Majuj will be let loose and they will emerge: as Allah Almighty says, *they will swarm down from every slope.*' (21:96) They will spread all over the earth and the Muslims will seek refuge from them until the remaining Muslims are confined to their cities and fortresses together with their flocks. When they pass by a river Yajuj and Majuj will drink it up so that there is nothing left in it. The last of them will follow in their tracks and say, 'There was once water in this place.'

"They will conquer the earth and will say, 'We have finished off the people of earth, so now let us fight the people of heaven!' One of them will throw his spear heavenwards and it will come back blood-stained. They will say, 'We have slain the people of heaven.' At this point Allah will send against them worm-like creatures in a swarm which will attack their necks and they will die *en masse*, falling on top of one another. In the morning the Muslims will hear no sound of them at all and will say, 'Is there any man who will sell himself to Allah and go and see what has happened to them?' A man will come down to them certain that they are going to kill him, but will find them dead. He will then call out to the people, 'Good news! Your enemy is destroyed!' People will come out and release their flocks which will have nothing to graze on except their flesh. They will be as grateful for that as they had been for the plants which they will no longer find at all." (Ibn Maja and Ahmad ibn Hanbal)

'Abdullah ibn Mas'ud, may Allah be pleased with him, narrated that the Messenger of Allah, may Allah bless him and grant him peace, said: "During the Night Journey, I met Ibrahim, Musa, and 'Isa, peace be upon them." In the *hadith* they discuss the Last Hour until 'Isa says, "When the Dajjal emerges, I will descend and kill him. People will return to their lands and be met by Yajuj and Majuj: *"When Yajuj and Majuj are let loose."* (21:96) Whenever they come to water, they will drink it up. Whenever they come upon anything, they will seize it. People will see refuge with Allah, and I will ask Allah to kill them and the earth will reek of their stench. Then I will pray to Allah and He will send rain, and it will carry them away and wash them into the sea.'" (Ibn Maja)

'Ali ibn Mu'abbad reported from al-Ash'ath from Shu'ba from Arta ibn al-Mundhir: "When Yajuj and Majuj emerge, Allah Almighty will reveal to 'Isa, peace be upon him, 'I have brought forth some slaves of Mine whom no one but I will be capable of fighting. Take those who are with you to Mount Tur.' There will be twelve thousand with him." Arta said, "Yajuj and Majuj are destined for Jahannam." (al-Qurtubi)

31

Zaynab bint Jahsh, may Allah be pleased with her, said that once when the Messenger of Allah, may Allah bless him and grant him peace, spent the night with her he woke up upset and said, "There is no god but Allah. Woe to the Arabs from an evil which is drawing near! Today an opening like this has been made in the wall of Yajuj and Majuj," and he made a circle with his thumb and forefinger. (Another variant says that he indicated the number seventy or ninety). She asked him, "O Messenger of Allah, will we be destroyed even though there are righteous people among us?" He said, "Yes, if wickedness is rife." (Al-Bukhari and Muslim)

Muhammad ibn Bashshar related the following from Muhammad ibn 'Amr ibn Harmala from his aunt: "The Messenger of Allah, may Allah bless him and grant him peace, once made a speech when he had his finger bandaged because of a scorpion sting and said, 'You say that you have no enemy. You will continue to have enemies to fight until Yajuj and Majuj emerge with broad faces, small eyes, and reddish brown skins, swarming down from every slope. Their faces look like shields covered with skins." (Ahmad ibn Hanbal)

Conclusion

I feel that this book would not be complete without a final section explaining the relevance of the information it contains to the people of the world we live in today. While undertaking the research required for this book, looking through the many books and manuscripts in which information about signs of the Hour and the appearance of the trials is to be found, I was struck by two inescapable conclusions.

Firstly, all these things spell good news for the people of belief and goodness in that Allah has chosen them by making them believers and, if they live until the signs appear, will take their souls by sending a good wind which no believer smells without dying instantly. That will take place before the Day of Rising and so Allah will save them from the terrors and afflictions of the Last Hour.

Secondly, these things are at the same time a terrible warning and the presage of an evil end for the people of disbelief and hypocrisy, communists and anti-religious people, and all those Jews and Christians who deny the realities of the Last Hour and the Day of Judgement. It is clear from the sources that the way of disbelief will be paramount in the world at the end of time, and it is the unbelievers who will face the Last Hour because, as the Prophet, may Allah bless him and grant him peace, told us, it will only come on confirmed unbelievers and base people and on people who do not mention Allah, and on the idolaters, who claim that there is some other god besides Allah.

There is a temptation for the believer to want to see these things happen and to see Allah's complete victory over all the forces of darkness and disbelief; to see the signs of the Hour when the Jews and Christians and unbelievers are confronted by them, so that his heart is healed and his anger appeased against the people of disbelief and misguidance; to see the people who reject Allah and His Messenger being made to pay for their arrogance; to see the Smoke enveloping them on every side and the Beast stamping their faces with rebellion and sealing them with unbelief or hypocrisy; to see the Dajjal capture and pervert them; to see Yajuj and Majuj consume their fresh and dry food and destroy their crops and animals; to hear Allah say to them, "You people of disbelief and misguidance, this is what you were promised! You worshippers of idols, this is the Book of Allah which will speak the truth against you!"

However, this is impossible: all we can do is ask Allah to put us among the people who have faith so that we may escape these terrible realities, and to make the people of our time pay heed to these things so that they come to recognise Allah and His Messenger before it is too late and they find themselves firstly face to face with them and then in the bottom of Jahannam with the Blazing Fire being kindled over them in the custody of Malik and the guardians of Hellfire, who will inflict an evil punishment on them and deprive them of anything to drink and remind them of the Words of Allah: *"We brought you the truth, but most of you were averse to the truth."* (43:78)

The people of our time must realise that all these things are true and will most certainly come about, and that a day is coming when Allah will overpower the people of disbelief and hypocrisy and the Jews and Christians of corrupt belief; a day when the earth will shake beneath their feet and their tongues become silent and their wits leave them; a day when they and their children and all their property will be inherited by the Muslims who have held firmly to their belief in Allah and all His Messengers.

The end of our supplication is: "Praise belongs to Allah, Lord of the worlds."

O Allah, bless our master Muhammad and his family and Companions.

Praise be to Allah by Whose blessing all righteous deeds are accomplished.

34

Bibliography

The Noble Qur'an

Ahmad 'Abdu'r-Rahman al-Banna, *al-Fath ar-Rabbani*, a commentary on the *Musnad* of Imam Ahmad ibn Hanbal

al-Bukhari, *Sahih al-Bukhari*

Ibn Hajar al-'Asqallani, *Fath al-Bari*, a commentary on the *Sahih al-Bukhari*

Ibn Kathir *Tafsir al-Qur'an al-Karim*

Ibn Kathir, *al-Bidaya wa'n-nihaya*

Layla Mabruk, *'Alamat as-Sa'at as-Sughra wa'l-Kubra*

Muslim, *Sahih Muslim*

an-Nawawi, *Sharh Sahih Muslim*

al-Qurtubi, *al-Jami' li-Ahkam al-Qur'an*

as-Sabuni, *Mukhtasar Tafsir Ibn Kathir*

Sayyid Qutb, *Fi Zilal al-Qur'an*

Shams'd-din al-Qurtubi, *at-Tadhkira fi ahwal al-mawta wa umur al-akhira.*

Yusuf 'Abdullah, *Ashrat as-Sa'a*

Brief biographies of some scholars mentioned in the text

'Abdu'r-Razzaq ibn Himam al-Himyari as-Sa'ani: He possessed great knowledge. Ahmad, Ishaq, Ibn Ma'in and adh-Dhihli all related from him. He went blind at the end of his life. He died in Shawwal, 211.

Abu 'Abdullah al-Hakim: the Imam of the meticulous scholars, Abu 'Abdullah Muhammad ibn 'Abdullah al-Hakim an-Nisaburi, known as Bab al-Bayyi'. He is the author of *al-Mustadrak*. He was born in 321 and died in Safar, 405. He heard lessons from about two thousand Shaykhs. His writings show his great fear of Allah.

Abu 'Awwan: the *hafiz* and *Hadith* scholar Ya'qub ibn Ishaq ibn Ibrahim an-Nisapuri then al-Isfara'ini. He was a leading scholar and the author of *al-Musnad as-Sahih al-Mukhrij 'ala Muslim*. He travelled all over the world in search of *Hadith*. He related from many people and many people related from him. He went on *hajj* five times and died in 316. His grave is in Isfara'in and is known and visited.

Abu Bakr ibn Abi Shayba: the exemplary author of the *Musnad*, *al-Musannif* and other books. Ibn Abi Shayba was a major authority in *Hadith*. Abu Zur'a, al-Bukhari, Muslim, and Abu Dawud all related from him. He died in Muharram, 235.

Abu Dawud: one of the greatest of the scholars of *Hadith*, Abu Sulayman ibn al-Ash'ath ibn Ishaq al-Azdi as-Sijistani, the author of the *Sunan*. He was born in 202 and died on a Friday in the middle of Shawwal, 275. He was so accomplished in the science of *Hadith* that it was said that *hadiths* were made pliable for Abu Dawud in the same way that iron was made pliable for the Prophet Dawud. He said, "I wrote down 500,000 *hadiths* of the Prophet and selected from them what those which are in the *Sunan*."

36

Abu Dawud at-Tayyalisi: Sulayman ibn Da'ud ibn al-Jarud al-Farisi. He was an outstanding scholar. Al-Qallas and Ibn al-Madini both said that they had never met anyone with a better memory than him. Ibn Mahdi said, "He is the most truthful of people." He wrote from a thousand shaykhs. He died in 204 at the age of eighty.

Abu Hatim ar-Razi: Muhammad ibn Idris This great Imam was born in 195 and died in Sha'ban, 277. He was skilled in the science of *Hadith*, especially in assessing their authenticity.

Abu 'Isa Muhammad ibn 'Isa at-Tirmidhi: Abu 'Isa Muhammad ibn 'Isa ibn Sura at-Tirmidhi, the author of *al-Jami'*. The name at-Tirmidhi derives from an ancient town on the eastern side of the Amu Darya. He was born in 209 and died on 13th Rajab, 279. It is said of his *Jami'*: "If anyone has it in his house, it is as if he had a speaking Prophet there." He was a student of al-Bukhari, who trained him. When al-Bukhari died there was no one else like Abu 'Isa in respect of knowledge, memorisation, scrupulousness and asceticism left in Khorasan. He went blind from weeping.

Abu Nu'aym al-Isbahani: the famous *hafiz* Ahmad ibn 'Abdullah ibn Ahmad al-Isbahani, a notable *Hadith* scholar who studied under many excellent men. He wrote various works, including *al-Mustadrak 'ala kull min as-Sahihayn.* and *Hilya al-Awliya'* which is one of the great books. It is said that it was taken to Nishapur and sold there for 400 dinars. He was born in Rajab, 334 and died in Safar, or on 20th Muharram, 340 in Isfahan.

Abu Ya'la: the *Hadith* scholar of Arabia, Ahmad ibn 'Ali ibn al-Muthanna at-Tamimi, author of the *Musnad al-Kabir*. He was known for his truthfulness, trustworthiness, *deen* and forbearance. As-Sam'ani stated, "I heard Isma'il ibn Muhammad say, 'I have read *Musnads* such as the *Musnad* of al-'Adani and the *Musnad* of Ibn Mani', and they are like rivers; but the *Musnad* of Abu Ya'la is like an ocean into which the rivers flow.'" He was born in Shawwal, 210 and died in 307.

Abu Zur'a ar-Razi: the great *Hadith* scholar, Abu Zur'a 'Ubaydullah ibn 'Abdu'l-Karim ar-Razi. He was a scholar and Imam in the science of criticism of authenticity. Muslim, at-Tirmidhi, an-Nasa'i, Ibn Maja and others related from him. Adh-Dhihli said, "He listened to many people in Makka and Madina, Iraq, Syria, Arabia, Khorasan and Egypt. He was one of the unique individuals of his time in respect of memory and intelligence, *deen*, sincerity, knowledge and action." He died in 264 at the age of 64.

Ahmad ibn 'Amr al-Bazzar: the famous Imam Abu Bakr Ahmad ibn 'Amr ibn 'Abdu'l-Khaliq al-Basri, the author of *Musnad al-Kabir* and *al-'Ilal*. He studied with at-Tabarani and others. He died in 292.

Ahmad ibn Hanbal: Abu 'Abdullah ibn Muhammad ibn Hanbal ash-Shaybani, one of the four Imams of the major schools of law. He was born in Rabi' al-Awwal, 164 and died on Friday 12 Rabi' al-Awwal, 241. Ahmad ibn Hanbal was the Imam who endured the greatest persecution. He is said to have memorised a million *hadiths*. It is said that on the day of his death 20,000 Christians, Jews and Zoroastrians became Muslim.

Ahmad ibn al-Husayn al-Bayhaqi: a famous scholar born in Sha'ban, 374 and died on 8th Jumada al-Ula, 457. His name comes from Bayhaq, a town near Nishapur. Al-Bayhaqi was one of the great Imams in *Hadith* and Shafi'i jurisprudence. He wrote some unparalleled books, such *as-Sunan al-Kubra*, *as-Sunan as-Sughra*, *al-Mabsut*, and *al-Asma' wa's-Sifat*.

'Ali ibn al-Madini: Abu'l-Hasan 'Ali ibn 'Abdullah as-Sa'id al-Madini, the Imam of *Hadith* criticism and one of the great men of *Hadith*. Al-Bukhari, Abu Dawud and others related from him. Ibn Mahdi said, "'Ali ibn al-Madini was the most knowledgeable of people concerning the *Hadith* of the Messenger of Allah." Al-Bukhari said, "I did not feel inferior to anyone except 'Ali ibn al-Madini." He was born in 161 and died in Samarra in the army of Qa'qa' in 234.

Ad-Daraqutni: Abu'l-Hasan 'Ali ibn 'Umar ad-Daraqutni, from Dar al-Qutn, a large district in Baghdad. This great Imam was born in 306 and died on 8th Dhu'l-Qa'da, 385. Ad-Daraqutni was unique in his time. He was foremost in the science of *Hadith* and in the recognition of faults in transmission and knowledge of transmitters in his time.

Ad-Darimi: the Imam and Shaykh al-Islam in Samarqand, Abu Muhammad 'Abdullah ibn 'Abdu'r-Rahman at-Tamimi ad-Darimi as-Samarqandi, author of the *Musnad*. He studied in Makka and Madina, Khorasan, Syria, Iraq and Egypt. Muslim, Abu Dawud, at-Tirmidhi, an-Nasa'i and others related from him. He had great intelligence and excellence. He was taken as an example of piety, forbearance, striving, worship and asceticism. He was born 181 and died in 255.

Ibn 'Abdu'l-Barr Yusuf ibn 'Abdullah: the famous Imam and Shaykh of Islam in the west, Abu 'Umar Yusuf ibn 'Abdullah ibn Muhammad ibn 'Abdu'l-Barr al-Qurtubi. 'Abdu'l-Barr was the master of the people of his time in memory and precision. He was an expert on genealogy and history. Ibn Hazm said, "There is no one with more knowledge of the *fiqh* of *Hadith* than he." He wrote a number of works, the most famous of which is *al-Isti'ab*. He was born in Rabi' al-Akhir, 368, and died in 463, at the age of 95.

Ibn Maja: one of the great scholars and Imams of *Hadith* was Abu 'Abdullah Muhammad ibn Yazid ibn Maja al-Qazwini, the author of the *Sunan*. He was born in 207 and died in Ramadan, 273 or 275. He studied under the companions of Malik and others. Many people related from him. His *Sunan* contains a great number of weak and even disliked *hadiths*.

Ibn al-Qattan: the perspicacious Imam, Abu'l-Hasan 'Ali ibn Muhammad al-Fa'si, born in Cordoba and lived in Fes. He was one of the people with the most insight into the science of *Hadith* and had the greatest retention of the names of its transmitters. He wrote *at-Ta'lif*. He was born in 562 and died in Rabi' al-Awwal, 628.

Ishaq ibn Rahawayh: the great Imam, Abu Ya'qub ibn Ibrahim at-Tamimi al-Hanzali al-Marwazi. He lived in Nishapur and was its greatest scholar. Indeed, he was the shaykh of the people of the east. Ahmad said, "I do not know of Ibn Rahawayh's equal in Iraq." Abu Zur'a said, "I never met anyone with a better memory than Ishaq." Abu Hatim said, "His precision and freedom from error is a marvel, besides the memory he was endowed with." He was born in 166 or 161 and died on the middle night of Sha'ban in 238.

Imam Malik: one of the four Imams to be followed in *fiqh*, the Imam of the Abode of the *Hijra*, the *faqih* of the community and the leader of the people of *Hadith*, Abu 'Abdullah Malik ibn Anas ibn Malik al-Asbahi. His lineage derives from Asbah, one of the noblest of the tribes of Yemen. He was born in 93 or 94 and died in Rabi' al-Awwal, 179. He studied under 900 or more shaykhs. He compiled that great record of the prophetic *Sunna*, *al-Muwatta'*. So many people transmitted from him that they cannot be counted. One of his students was Imam ash-Shafi'i.

Muhammad ibn Ishaq ibn Khuzayma: the Shaykh al-Islam, one of the great scholars, born in 223 in Nishapur and died in 311. He was the Imam of his time in Khorasan. He wrote more than 140 books.

Muhammad ibn Isma'il al-Bukhari: the leader of the believers in the field of *Hadith*. His full name was Abu 'Abdullah Muhammad ibn Isma'il ibn Ibrahim ibn al-Mughira al-Ju'fi al-Bukhari. He was born in Shawwal 194 and died on the night of the *'Id al-Fitr* in 156. He was a marvel in the science of *Hadith*. His book, *al-Jami' as-Sahih,* is the soundest of books after the Book of Allah.

Muslim ibn al-Hajjaj: one of the famous Imams. His full name is Muslim ibn al-Hajjaj al-Qushayri an-Nisaburi. He was born in 204 and died in Rajab, 261. His book, *al-Jami' as-Sahih*, is the soundest of books after the *Sahih* of al-Bukhari. He listened to al-Bukhari and other great Imams of *Hadith*.

An-Nasa'i: Abu 'Abdu'r-Rahman Ahmad ibn 'Ali ibn Shu'ayb ibn 'Ali, the author of *as-Sunan al-Mujtaba*. His name is taken from Nasa, a city in Khorasan. He was born in 215 and died in 303. He was skilled in the science of *Hadith* and unique in memorisation and precision. His *Sunan* is the one with the fewest weak *hadiths* after the two *Sahih* collections. He lived in Egypt and then moved to Damascus, where he wrote the *Kitab al-Khasa'is fi fadl 'Ali*. They treated him badly there and finally expelled him from the mosque. Then he was taken to Makka where he died.

Imam ash-Shafi'i: one of the Imams with a school of *fiqh*. His full name was Abu 'Abdullah Muhammad ibn Idris al-Qurashi al-Makki. He lived in Egypt. He was born in 250 at Anaza and was carried to Makka. He died in 294 in Egypt. Ash-Shafi'i was the matchless scholar of the community, the most knowledgeable of people in the east and west. He was skilled in all branches of knowledge and founded the science of the foundations of *fiqh*.

At-Tabarani: Imam Abu'l-Qasim Sulayman ibn Ahmad al-Lakhmi at-Tabarani. He related from a thousand or more shaykhs. He travelled from Syria in quest of *Hadith,* and his journey lasted 33 years. At-Tabarani compiled some outstanding books, including three lexicons: *al-Kabir, al-Awsat* and *as-Saghir*. He was born in 260 in Syria and lived in Isfahan, where he died at the end of Dhu'l-Qa'da, 360.

At-Tahawi: Imam Abu Ahmad ibn Muhammad al-Misri at-Tahawi al-Hanafi. Taha is a village in Egypt. He began as a Shafi'i studying with al-Muzni, who was his uncle. One day al-Muzni said to him, "By Allah, you have achieved nothing." At-Tahawi became angry and went to Ibn Abi 'Imran al-Hanafi and became a Hanafi, so eager to establish that school that he demanded the transmission of reports of history according to his school and using what others considered to be weak arguments, according to al-Bayhaqi. One of his most famous works is the *Commentary on the Meanings of Traditions*. He was born in 228 and died in Dhu'l-Qa'da, 321.

Al-'Uqayli: Imam Abu Ja'far Muhammad ibn 'Amr ibn Musa al-'Uqayli, author of the *Kitab ad-Du'afa' al-Kabir*. He was a very eminent scholar and wrote many books. He lived in Makka and Madina, and died in 322.